Supporting Children with
Asthma

Hull Learning Services

 David Fulton Publishers

David Fulton Publishers Ltd
The Chiswick Centre, 414 Chiswick High Road, London W4 5TF

www.fultonpublishers.co.uk

First published in Great Britain by Hull Learning Services

Note: The right of the author to be identified as the author of this work has been asserted by him in accordance with the Copyright, Designs and Patents Act 1988.

David Fulton Publishers is a division of Granada Learning Limited, part of ITV plc.

Copyright © David Fulton Publishers 2004

British Library Cataloguing in Publication Data
A catalogue record for this book is available from the British Library.

ISBN 1 84312 218 9

Typeset by Matrix Creative, Wokingham
Printed and bound in Great Britain

Contents

Foreword

This book was produced in partnership with the Educational Service for Physical Disability (ESPD), Hull; the Special Educational Needs Support Service (SENSS) and the Paediatric Asthma Task Force, Hull.

It was written by:

Susan Coulter (ESPD)
Elizabeth Morling (SENSS)
Daryl Parks (Paediatric Specialist Asthma Nurse)

It is one of a series of eleven titles providing an up-to-date overview of special educational needs for Special Educational Needs Co-ordinators (SENCOs), teachers, classroom assistants and other professionals, and parents.

The aim of this book is to raise awareness and address many of the issues involved in supporting children with asthma in schools, following guidance given by the National Asthma Campaign.

In recognition of heavy workloads and a limited amount of time for reading, the authors present information and guidance in a concise way that is straightforward and instantly accessible. SENCOs may find it useful to copy some of the pages for distributing to other members of staff and/or for saving time on developing their own policy and record keeping systems.

For details of other titles and how to order, please see p.35.

Acknowledgements

We would like to extend our thanks to the Hull and East Riding Paediatric Asthma Task Force for their guidance and support in producing this booklet.

We would like to thank senior adviser John Hill for his support and encouragement throughout the development of this series.

Introduction

The majority of pupils with asthma are educated in their local mainstream schools. The condition is such that pupils can usually access the full curriculum when consideration is given to their individual medical needs. A small number of pupils who have asthma may be educated in a special school environment; however, asthma is unlikely to be their primary special educational need.

"A medical diagnosis ... does not necessarily imply SEN... It is the child's educational needs rather than diagnosis that must be considered." 7:64 SENDA 2001

Children with asthma come within the remit of the Special Educational Needs and Disability Act 2001 (SENDA 2001) when their condition *'has a substantial and long-term adverse affect on his or her ability to carry out normal day-to-day activities'.* Not all children fall within this description; however, schools have a duty to anticipate the needs of all children with asthma.

"A person has a disability... if he has a physical or mental impairment that has a substantial and long-term adverse affect on his ability to carry out normal day-to-day activities." Section 1(1), Disability Discrimination Act 1995

Implications of the Disability Discrimination Act (1995) as amended by the Special Educational Needs and Disability Act 2001 (SENDA 2001)

Part one of the Act

- strengthens the right of children to be educated in mainstream schools;
- requires LEAs to arrange for parents and/or children with SEN to be provided with advice on SEN matters, and also a means of settling disputes with schools and LEAs (parent partnership services and mediation schemes);
- requires schools to tell parents where they are making special educational provision for their child and allows schools to request a statutory assessment of a pupil's needs.

In accordance with the above Act LEAs and schools must:

- not treat disabled pupils less favourably;
- make reasonable adjustments so that the physical, sensory and learning needs of disabled pupils are accommodated, in order that they are not put at a substantial disadvantage to pupils who are not disabled;
- plan strategically and make progress in increasing not only physical accessibility to the schools' premises and to the curriculum, but also to improve the delivery of written information in an accessible way to disabled pupils (i.e. access to the curriculum via oral means, as well as the written word).

Triggers for asthma

A trigger is anything that irritates the airway and causes symptoms of asthma to appear. Everybody is different and may react to one or more triggers. Some of the more common triggers are listed here:

- colds, flu and other viral infections;
- house dust mite;
- cigarette smoking/passive smoking;
- fur and feathers;
- pollen;
- exercise.

Other triggers for asthma can be:

- Mould/spores;
- changes in weather;
- changes in emotion – laughter, crying;
- effects of chemicals, paints, car fumes, spray deodorants, etc.;
- hormones, especially during puberty;
- stress.

How to recognise an attack

Symptoms of an asthma attack may include the following:

- Breathlessness
- Wheezing
- Coughing
- Complaining of chest tightness/shortness of breath

An attack which is worsening and needs urgent medical attention may have some or all of the above plus:

- difficulty in speaking;
- a blue tinge around the lips;
- the person involved is becoming exhausted;
- pulse and breathing rate are increased.

Action

1. Stay calm.
2. Sit the pupil in an upright position.
3. Encourage the pupil to breathe slowly and calmly.
4. Follow the flow chart (over the page) to administer reliever inhaler.
5. If you have any doubts about the pupil's condition call an ambulance.

What to do if a pupil is having an asthma attack

Your aims are:
>
> to ease breathing;
> to seek medical aid if necessary.

1.   Keep calm and reassure the pupil.
2.   Let the pupil adopt the position he/she finds most comfortable; this is usually sitting down.
3.   Follow the guidelines below for administering treatment:

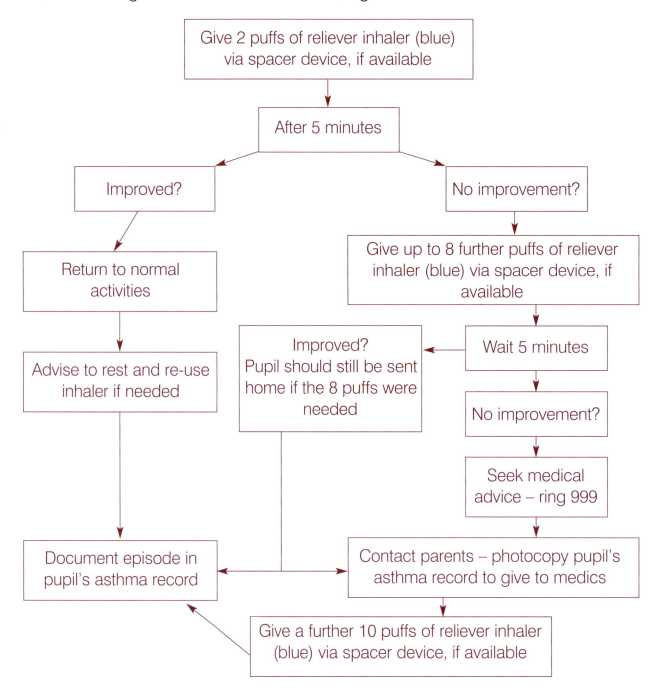

Action to take if an inhaler is missing, forgotten, empty...

- The drug and dosage is common to all blue inhalers irrespective of their shape, size or design.

- In an emergency, it is completely safe to allow a pupil whose inhaler is not available to use one belonging to another pupil.

- Clean the mouthpiece before and after use; record the incident in the pupil's asthma record.

- If the above situation occurs, parents should be notified and a replacement inhaler requested.

Management of inhalers

- Instant access to inhalers is vital.
- Inhalers should always be visible, never locked away.
- Inhalers must be labelled by the parent with the pupil's name.
- All pupils should be encouraged to manage their own inhalers. If schools do not find this arrangement acceptable then the following recommendations are made:

Key Stage One

- Inhalers should be kept in a prominent place within the classroom and should be taken by a member of staff when pupils move between classrooms.
- Consideration should be given to availability of inhalers during breaks, lunch time and PE lessons if they are not carried by the pupil.
- Younger pupils could carry their inhalers in a bum bag, belt bag or wrist bag to ensure safe keeping.

Key Stage Two and above

- Inhalers should be carried by the pupils at all times.
- Staff are not generally required to administer inhalers as they are intended to be self administered.
- If pupils become distressed and do not recover within 5–10 minutes of using their inhalers they may need adult support (see flow chart page 6).

Treatments for asthma

The treatment of asthma can be divided into three main groups:

- Relievers
- Controllers
- Protectors

Note: *Only 'blue' inhalers are required in school.*

Relievers

- These are usually blue in colour and come in a range of devices.
- They are used to relieve symptoms when they occur (they usually take effect within 5–10 minutes).
- Two puffs of a reliever can be used 5–10 minutes before exercise to prevent symptoms occurring.
- Relievers must be carried by the person at all times or be readily available for Key Stage One pupils.
- The medicine in reliever inhalers will not cause problems if taken by another person. Neither the propellant nor the drug is addictive.

Controllers

- These come in a range of devices and are usually coloured brown, orange or red depending on the medicine it contains.
- Controllers reduce swelling in the airways and stop them being so sensitive. Regular use of a preventer will reduce the risk of a severe attack.
- Controllers medicine needs to be taken regularly, usually twice a day and must be continued until advised otherwise by the doctor.
- The steroids used in controllers inhalers are not the same as those used by body builders. The dose is very small and works directly in the lung where it is needed.

Protectors

- Protectors are relatively new in the treatment of asthma.
- They act in a similar way to relievers but the drug has a longer lasting effect.
- They come in two forms:
  - Inhaler (usually green) which is taken twice a day. This inhaler should never be used as a reliever inhaler.
  - Tablet form which is taken either once or twice daily depending on the drug, in addition to inhaler therapy.

Inhaler techniques

Metered Dose Inhaler

1. Remove the cap from the mouthpiece.
2. Shake the inhaler.
3. Breathe out slowly.
4. Place the mouthpiece between the lips and start to breathe in slowly. Press the canister and continue to breathe in as deeply and as evenly as possible.
5. Hold your breath for as long as is comfortable.
6. Repeat the procedure 30–60 seconds later, if another inhalation is required.

Accuhaler

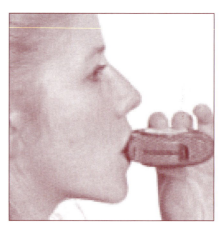

1. Hold the outer casing and push the thumb grip until it 'clicks'.
2. Slide the lever until it 'clicks'.
3. Breathe out fully.
4. Holding the Accuhaler level put the mouthpiece in the mouth and take a deep breath in.
5. Remove Accuhaler from the mouth and hold breath for 10 seconds.
6. Close Accuhaler by sliding the thumb grip until it closes.
7. Repeat if necessary.

Turbohaler

1. Remove the lid by unscrewing it from the device.
2. Hold the Turbohaler upright and turn the bottom grip clockwise and then anti-clockwise until a click is heard.
3. Breathe out slowly and deeply.
4. Place inhaler in mouth and seal the lips around.
5. Holding the Turbohaler horizontally breathe in as deeply as possible.
6. Hold your breath for as long as is comfortable, 10 seconds ideally.
7. Repeat from 2 if necessary.

Large Volume Spacer

1. Fit the two pieces of the spacer together.

2. Remove the cap from the inhaler. Shake the inhaler well.

3. Fit the inhaler into the opening of the spacer.

4. Place the mouthpiece of the spacer into the mouth, making sure the lips are sealed behind the ring. Press the canister once and breathe in and out slowly and deeply for 15–20 seconds.

5. Remove the spacer from the mouth and repeat the procedure from step 2 for each dose of the drug.

Educational issues

Consider the following general points:

- All staff should be familiar with the school policy on storage of inhalers.
- All staff should be aware of the Asthma Policy and refer to it when necessary.
- The Asthma Register should be used to share accurate information to all staff.
- Establish a clear referral route through the pastoral system to ensure teachers' concerns are passed to the parents and the school nurse.
- All classrooms should be adequately ventilated.
- Pupils should be allowed to position themselves out of direct sunlight.
- White boards should be used, rather than chalk boards, to avoid creation of dust.
- Pupils should be given access to water in all lessons to help them deal with coughing episodes.

Primary schools:

- Wash soft toys and soft furnishings regularly to destroy dust mites.
- Keep carpeted areas clear to allow for thorough vacuuming.
- Provide a play area away from newly cut grass when pollen counts are high.

If health problems occur:

Staff should be aware that coughing, tiredness and reduced physical activity in pupils with asthma can result from poor symptom control. These symptoms may be an indication that the pupil's medication is not working effectively.

If a member of staff has concerns about the progress of a pupil with asthma he/she should discuss this with the relevant pastoral staff so that concerns can be passed on to the parent and/or the school nurse.

It is not normally necessary to inform parents that their child has used his/her inhaler during the school day.

Staff should be aware that if pupils are able to return to normal activities, within 5–10 minutes of using two puffs of the inhaler, this is an indication that his/her condition is being managed well by the current medication.

Strategies to compensate for frequent asthma related absences

Statistics show that many more than a third of children who have asthma miss more than a week from school each year. Some miss as much as a month of schooling due to asthma related illness. The following strategies are suggested to help teachers ensure that pupils are able to catch up.

- Pupil should nominate a reliable 'buddy' in each lesson to pass on lesson notes following an absence.

- Establish a system to allow named pupils to access the school photocopier to copy missed lesson notes on return to school. Ensure that relevant administrative staff are aware of this agreement.

- Teachers to maintain a file of handouts provided in lessons for pupils to access on their return.

- Teachers to post lesson outlines, handouts and homework on the school's internet website to enable pupils to access work from their home computers.

- School to organise departmental 'catch up clubs' alongside 'homework clubs' to offer support to pupils who have been absent due to illness.

- Ensure that information regarding field trips, etc. is provided for pupils who are absent when it is distributed.

Emotional issues

The following comments have been made by young people with asthma. They give an insight into the typical areas of concern and the emotional issues that they have to deal with.

Young people may not always want to, or be able to, express their feelings verbally; however, today's pupil is likely to be confident and competent in communicating non-verbally via text messaging and internet chat rooms.

In the Hull and East Riding of Yorkshire Health Area the specialist asthma nurse gives her mobile phone number to students on the school asthma register so that they can text concerns to her. In addition the school nurse holds a regular drop-in asthma clinic. Pupils are able to self-refer to the clinic; staff are also able to refer pupils through the pastoral head of year.

Sleep deprivation

"I've been waking up at 1am and then 3am; I fall back asleep but when I get up I still have a hoarse cough and I feel out of it. I don't know why this is happening cos I take my reliever inhaler before I go to bed… What should I do? I need my sleep for school. This has been happening for the last three years."

Smoking

"Whatever you say smoking will affect your asthma. When I was younger I gave up (smoking) when I ended up in hospital for a week on oxygen and now I can't go in a smoky pub cos I need to use my nebuliser cos my chest gets so tight."

Smoking and school transport

"I've just started at a new school and there are lots of older kids on the school bus who smoke and it really affects me. My chest gets painful and I'm frightened that I'll have a really bad attack one day and nobody will know me… They aren't allowed to smoke on the school bus but they do anyway and the bus driver doesn't do anything about it."

PE and Games

"I am a keen athlete and I don't think asthma should stop you doing the things you enjoy. I get really frustrated when I have a bad patch and don't perform as well as I usually can."

"In PE I always get picked last and people shout at me when I get tired or when they pass a ball to me and I can't kick it. I try to get out of PE if I can."

Symptom control

"Sometimes in the middle of my lessons I start coughing because of my asthma. It wouldn't be so bad if it didn't sound like a bark! Everyone stares at me, even the teachers. It's so embarrassing."

Working effectively with parents

Parents need to be confident that their child who has asthma will:

- be happy and safe within school;
- be able to take part in all school activities;
- have instant access to their inhalers;
- be given appropriate support if they have an asthma attack;
- be encouraged to manage their asthma as independently as possible;
- be able to seek help and further advice from a named person within school.

Parents will be reassured if they know that all staff:

- have an understanding of how asthma affects children in school;
- know which pupils in their classes have asthma;
- know what the possible triggers for asthma can be;
- know how to recognise an asthma attack;
- know what to do when a pupil has an asthma attack;
- will listen to their concerns relating to their child's asthma and how it affects their child in school.

Specific subject advice

Physical Education

Exercise is a very important part of life and having asthma should not exclude anyone from participating fully. However, the following points may help to ensure that pupils with asthma get the most out of exercise:

- ensure the pupil with asthma is fully involved in the warm up session – 5–10 minutes is recommended;
- using 2 puffs of a reliever inhaler prior to exercise may help prevent symptoms occurring if exercise is known to be a trigger;
- be aware that some types of exercise are more likely to induce symptoms, e.g. cross-country running on a cold day (consider providing an alternative activity);
- always allow pupils to carry their reliever (blue) inhaler throughout PE lessons.

PE staff should be aware that pupils with asthma rarely use their condition as an excuse not to participate. Try to consider the possible reasons why a pupil is reluctant to participate in PE lessons. Is it health related or peer pressure related?

Allow pupils with asthma to be self-limiting where possible. Asthma can be a fluctuating condition, therefore it is not always possible for parents to provide a note excusing their child from PE.

Try to group pupils sensitively so that pupils with asthma are not always left until last when teams or partners are picked.

Ensure activities are suitably differentiated to allow all pupils to participate at their own level of competency and level of tolerance to exercise.

Design and Technology

Flour, icing sugar, wood dust and clay dust can all trigger symptoms if inhaled. Dust masks may be required when working with resistant materials.

Science

Be aware that smoke and fumes can trigger symptoms for some pupils with asthma. Ensure adequate ventilation.

Art

Spray paints, powder paints, plaster of Paris and chalks may trigger symptoms. Use with care unless contrary advice is given regarding a specific pupil. Consider using alternative media.

Out of school visits

Pupils with asthma should be included in all out of school activities unless specifically advised otherwise by the GP/parents. The following arrangements should be in place:

- a risk assessment which considers the implications of contact with potential triggers for asthma. Refer to pages 4 and 19 for guidance on triggers;
- ensure that the reliever inhaler is readily available to the pupil at all times, either being carried by the pupil or for younger pupils by the adult supervising the group;
- group leaders on residential trips should be trained in the prevention of asthma as well as the emergency treatment;
- accompanying staff should be aware of potential triggers for individual pupils within their group;
- appropriate contact numbers should be carried.

Animals

Exercise caution when arranging activities which bring pupils into contact with animals, particularly cats and dogs. Check with the pupil and/or parents whether this is a trigger for their child.

Specialist careers advice

Members of staff who are responsible for work experience and careers guidance should be familiar with contra-indications related to asthma in the workplace. Pupils with asthma should be made aware that there are some careers which they will not be able to consider:

- The Ambulance Service will not accept people with asthma.
- The Fire Service will not employ people with asthma.
- The Armed Forces did not accept anyone who had asthma at the time of applying; the application process has changed and entrance standards are now less strict; contact the British Army, tel: 08457 300 111 or www.army.mod.uk for careers advice.
- The Royal Air Force/Aviation will not allow anyone who has had asthma to fly.
- The Police Force does not have a national policy on accepting candidates with asthma. Applications are considered individually at a local level.
- The Prison Service requires applicants to undertake a comprehensive medical and fitness test. Contact the Prison Officer Recruitment Helpline (0870 892 2289) or www.hmprisonservice.gov.uk
- The Royal Navy and Royal Marines require applicants to be physically fit and to pass a medical examination. Information is available on line at www.royal-navy.mod.uk

It is unlikely that a person who has mild asthma will experience problems when applying for a job. Applicants have a duty to disclose if they have asthma; pupils should be sure to say if their asthma is well controlled and emphasise whether or not attendance at school has been affected.

The table opposite lists possible triggers which can cause occupational asthma or irritate existing asthma. It should be noted that employers can protect their workforce in a number of ways including:

- fitting extractor fans;
- provision of masks and protective clothing;
- sealing off any equipment which produces hazardous substances from the air they breathe.

Workplace	Possible triggers in the workplace
Office/Clerical work	Photocopier fumes Fumes from new furniture Passive smoking – communal areas
Agriculture, farming and veterinary science	Hay Pesticides Pollen Dust from flour and grain Animal fur Animal urine
Medicine, dentistry and pharmaceuticals	Dust from latex gloves Anaesthetic gases Disinfectants Production of antibiotics Latex allergy (use vinyl as alternative)

Engineering	Fumes from:
	  – chemicals;
	  – welding materials;
	  – spray paints;
	  – metals;
	  – resins.

Textile industry	Fibres from:
	  – cotton;
	  – flax;
	  – hemp.

Food science and technology	Fish Spices Flour
Beauty therapy and hairdressing	Chemical substances in hair and beauty products, e.g. henna Fumes from bleach and dye
Building, carpentry and decorating	Wood dust Chemicals Cleaning products Paint and varnish Resins House dust mite
Gardening and floristry	Pollen Chemicals Pesticides
Hospitality	Contact with smoke in public areas House dust mites Cleaning products

School staff: duties and responsibilities

Staff often have concerns regarding their obligation to administer medicines in school. The following advice is given by the DfEE/DH:

"Employers (usually the LEA or governing body) should ensure that their insurance policies provide appropriate cover for staff willing to support pupils with medical needs." para. 13

"Subject to this point, there is no legal or contractual duty on staff to administer medicine or supervise a pupil taking it. This is a voluntary role. Support staff may have specific duties to provide medical assistance as part of their contract." para. 13

"Teachers and other school staff have a common law duty to act as any reasonably prudent parent would to make sure pupils are healthy and safe on school premises and this might in exceptional circumstances extend to administering medicine and/or taking action in an emergency." para. 14

It is usual for schools to identify staff who are willing to carry out these duties on a voluntary basis.

DfEE/DH circular 14/96 "Supporting Pupils with Medical Needs in Schools."

School policy

Schools are responsible for ensuring that they have an appropriate policy to meet the needs of pupils who have asthma. The policy should be clearly understood by the LEA, governors, teaching and non-teaching staff, parents and pupils.

The policy should be written by the head teacher in consultation with the SENCO and school nurse or specialist support nurse. It should be a stand alone document which should be referred to in the Special Educational Needs Policy and the Health and Safety Policy. The policy statement should recognise that:

- asthma and recurrent wheezing are important conditions affecting many school children;
- the school welcomes pupils with these conditions;
- the school will encourage pupils with asthma to achieve their full potential in all aspects of school life.

The pupils should be made aware of a 'named person' to whom they can turn when they have concerns.

School transport contractors should be made aware of pupils with asthma who travel on school buses. It is a parental responsibility to ensure that this information is provided to the LEA and the individual contractor.

See Appendix 4 for an example of a school policy.

Admission procedure

A question related to asthma and recurrent wheezing should be included in the school's admission form.

- Parents who state that their child has this condition should be asked more detailed questions related to the condition and the required treatment (see Appendices 2 and 3 for a sample 'letter to parents' and 'Asthma record').
- The pupil's name should be added to the School Asthma Register.
- The completed form should then be stored in the school's recording system.
- The information should be updated by parents or when medication is changed.

Dissemination of information

- The asthma register should be drawn to the attention of all school staff.
- It should be displayed prominently in a central area, e.g. the school office and/or the staff room.
- All staff should know where medication is stored.
- All school staff should be trained at regular intervals by the school nurse.
- Visiting staff, e.g. supply teachers should be made aware of pupils whose names appear on the asthma register. They should be informed of the school's procedure for the storage of inhalers.

Raising awareness about asthma

Given the high incidence of asthma in children of school age it is important that parents, staff and pupils are kept informed of current practices and developments.

The following model was used by the Hull and East Riding Health Trust in conjunction with the Kingston upon Hull and East Riding of Yorkshire Education Authorities and Social Services to enhance provision for children with asthma.

The Paediatric Asthma Task Force, made up of representatives from a variety of disciplines including consultant paediatricians, specialist asthma nurse, GP, practice nurse, social worker, pharmacist, public health consultant, health promotion teacher, support teacher for pupils with physical disabilities and a housing officer, aimed to improve provision for children with asthma in the local area.

Their work resulted in:

- the production of a school policy which has been adopted by the Local Education Authorities;
- provision of school-based training, for teachers and support assistants, in the management of asthma in schools;
- awareness of asthma being raised by involving schools through the use of questionnaires, poetry, art and design competitions;
- production of a puppet show which is taken 'on tour' by the specialist support nurse;
- promotion of asthma related activities in the local media;
- contributions being made to national educational publications.

Useful contacts

Further information/advice about all aspects of asthma and its management can be obtained from either of the following:

National Asthma Campaign
Providence House
Providence Place
London N1 0NT
www.asthma.org.uk

Paediatric Asthma Task Force
c/o The Children's Centre
Walker Street
Hull HU3 2HE

Your own school nurse Name:...

Contact number: ....

Reading list

Books for children

Alden J, (1992) *A Boy's Best Friend*, Alyson Publications

Carter A R, (1999) *I'm Tougher Than Asthma!* Concept Publishers

Charlton M, (1988) *Wheezy*, Bodley Head Children's Books

Condon J, (1998) *When It's Hard to Breathe*, Franklin Watts

Gosselin K *et al*, (1998) *The ABC's of Asthma: An Asthma Alphabet Book for Kids of All Ages*, Jay Jo Publishers

Gosselin K *et al*, (1998) *Taking Asthma to School (Special Kids in Schools)*, 2nd Edition, Jay Jo Publishers

Gosselin K *et al*, (1998) *Zooallergy: A Fun Story About Allergy and Asthma Triggers*, Jay Jo Publishers

London J, (1997) *The Lion Who Had Asthma*, Concept Publishers

Sutherland S, (1987) *Help Me, Mummy I Can't Breathe: Coping with Childhood Asthma (Human Horizons)*, Souvenir Press

Weiss J, (2003) *Breathe Easy: Young People's Guide to Asthma*, 2nd edition, Magination Publishers

Books for parents/carers

Farber H & Boyette M (2001) *Control Your Child's Asthma*, Henry Holt & Company

May J (2001) *My House Is Killing Me: The Home Guide for Families with Allergies and Asthma*, Johns Hopkins University Press

Issues for consideration

Issue for consideration	✓	✗	Action required (examples)
Is the Governing Body aware of the educational implications of asthma and its responsibilities in ensuring that those needs are met?			Contact specialist asthma nurse to arrange asthma training for governors
Is there a policy to address the needs of the pupil with asthma?			Liaise with school nurse to write policy using example from this book for guidance
Are all staff aware of the management of the pupil's medication?			Circulate policy for reading
Are all staff appropriately trained?			Arrange staff INSET, review annually
Have pupils with asthma been identified?			Photograph of each pupil with asthma displayed on a notice board in the staff room
Has the school ensured that supply staff are made aware of pupils with asthma?			Supply staff induction folder in use
Are effective methods of ensuring communication between home and school in place?			Establish asthma record. Establish communication route to parents
Is there a mechanism in place for updating all asthma records annually?			Identify review of asthma records in school planner
Are any other agencies involved in supporting pupils with asthma?			School nurse number: _____ Specialist nurse number: _____
Do pupils know how to seek advice from the school nurse?			Nurse's mobile phone number displayed in Medical Room and Form notice boards. Pastoral staff to raise awareness of their role
Is there a named member of the school staff who has responsibility for managing the Asthma Policy and implementation in school?			Nominate a member of staff
Do staff know where to seek further information and advice?			www.epilepsy.org.uk Asthma resource bank – teachers' library
Are there any curriculum areas which may require particular consideration, e.g. PE?			Arrange additional INSET for PE staff Liaison with professional body Liaison with subject adviser
Have parents been made aware of their duty to inform the LEA/transport provider of their child's condition?			Note to parents regarding transport issues

Issues for consideration

Issue for consideration	✓	✗	Action required (examples)
Is the Governing Body aware of the educational implications of asthma and its responsibilities in ensuring that those needs are met?			
Is there a policy to address the needs of the pupil with asthma?			
Are all staff aware of the management of the pupil's medication?			
Are all staff appropriately trained?			
Have pupils with asthma been identified?			
Has the school ensured that supply staff are made aware of pupils with asthma?			
Are effective methods of ensuring communication between home and school in place?			
Is there a mechanism in place for updating all asthma records annually?			
Are any other agencies involved in supporting pupils with asthma?			
Do pupils know how to seek advice from the school nurse?			
Is there a named member of the school staff who has responsibility for managing the Asthma Policy and implementation in school?			
Do staff know where to seek further information and advice?			
Are there any curriculum areas which may require particular consideration, e.g. PE?			
Have parents been made aware of their duty to inform the LEA/transport provider of their child's condition?			

Request for additional information

Dear Parent/Carer

We know that you, as the parent/carer of a child who suffers from asthma, or who has a problem with wheezing which requires treatment with an inhaler, are keen to ensure that your child receives the best possible care for this whilst in school.

This school takes its responsibilities seriously and has a School Asthma Policy in place for use by all staff. In order for us to manage your child's condition effectively, we are asking all parents/carers of affected children to complete a confidential asthma record form. It will contain details of your child's current treatment, emergency contact numbers for our use and outlines your responsibilities to ensure that your child's condition is well managed.

Please complete the enclosed form and return it to me within 2 weeks. It will be held by the school and you will be asked to complete it once a year, or sooner if your child's treatment changes. Thank you for your co-operation.

Yours sincerely

Head teacher

Asthma record

CONFIDENTIAL
MEDICAL RECORD – ASTHMA RECORD

Name of Child:.. Date of Birth:................................

Name of Parent/Carer: ....

Address:..

.... Tel: ....

GP Name: ....

& Address: ....

....

Emergency contacts

1. Name: .... 2. Name: ....

   Address: .... Address: ....

   ....

   ....

   Tel No: .... Tel No:...

   Relationship to child: .... Relationship to child: ....

Storage (Please tick)

I would be happy for my child's inhaler to be kept:

   By my child   ☐

   By the teacher in the classroom   ☐

I agree to undertake the following to ensure my child's asthma is best controlled in school:

1. I will provide an inhaler for my child, clearly labelled with his/her name and class.

2. I will regularly check that there is enough medication for my child and provide a new inhaler as soon as it is needed.

3. I will update this record card once a year.

4. I will inform school if any changes are made to my child's medication.

Signed: .... **Date:**....................................

         (Parent/Carer)

School Asthma and Inhaler Policy

This policy has been written with advice from the National Asthma Campaign, Department of Education and Employment and healthcare professionals.

Policy statement

This school recognises that asthma and recurrent wheezing are important conditions affecting many school children, and welcomes pupils with these conditions.

This school encourages children with asthma to achieve their full potential in all aspects of life by having a clear policy that is understood by school staff, their employers and pupils.

All staff who have contact with children with asthma are given the opportunity to receive training from the school nursing team. This training is updated at regular intervals.

Medication

Immediate access to inhalers is vital. Children are encouraged to carry their inhalers with them, at the discretion of the parent/teacher and depending on the maturity of the child. As a guideline we would recommend that:

Key Stage 1   Inhalers will be kept by the teacher in the classroom in a designated place, of which pupils will be made aware.

Key Stage 2   Inhalers will be kept by the pupil.
(and above)

All inhalers will be labelled by the parent with the child's name. Many children will identify for themselves the need to take their medication, and should be allowed to do so, as and when they feel it is necessary.

School staff are not required to administer medication, as it is self-administered. However, in an emergency it may become necessary to assist the child to take his/her medication. Staff who agree to do this, and act in accordance with this policy and its allied guidelines, will be insured by the Local Education Authority.

Record keeping

When a child joins the school, parents/guardians are asked if their child has asthma/recurrent wheezing. They are asked to complete a form giving details of the condition and the treatment required. Information from this form is used to compile an 'Asthma Register', which is available for all school staff. This form will be updated annually by the parents and in between times if medication changes are made.

Physical Education

Taking part in sports is an essential part of school life and children with asthma/recurrent wheezing are encouraged to participate fully in PE.

Symptoms of asthma are often brought on by exercise and therefore, each child's labelled inhaler will be available at the site of the lesson.

Certain types of exercise are potent triggers for asthma/recurrent wheezing, e.g. cross-country running. Any child who knows that this type of exercise does bring on symptoms, will be allowed to take an inhaler prior to exercise, carry it with him/her throughout and will be encouraged to gently warm up before the exercise.

School trips

No child will be denied the opportunity to take part in school trips/holidays because of asthma/recurrent wheezing, unless so advised by their GP.

Their reliever inhaler will be readily available throughout the trip, being carried either by the child or by the supervising adult whichever is more appropriate.

Group leaders need to be trained in the prevention of asthma, as well as the emergency management. They will have appropriate contact numbers with them.

Education

This school will be encouraged and supported by the School Health Care Team to include asthma education for pupils. This teaching will be allied to the Key Stages and therefore appropriate to their level of understanding.

Problems

If the teacher has concerns about the progress of an asthmatic child, which he/she feels may be related to poor symptom control, he/she will be encouraged to discuss this with the parent and/or school nurse.

Storage

The following good practice guidelines will be followed:

1. Inhalers will NEVER be locked away.
2. All children with asthma will have rapid access to their devices.
3. Devices will always be taken with the children when moving out of their classroom, e.g. science rooms, school trips, PE classes, and art & technology rooms.

Emergency procedures

Guidelines are issued along with this policy outlining the action to take in an emergency. A copy is kept with other school health policies and is available for all to read on request.

Improve your support for pupils with SEN with other books in this series...

The books in this series gather together all the vital knowledge and practical support that schools need to meet specific special needs. Information is simply explained and clearly sign-posted so that practitioners can quickly access what they need to know. Each book describes a specific area of special educational need and explains how it might present difficulties for pupils within the school setting. Checklists and photocopiable forms are provided to help save time and develop good practice.

Supporting Children with Behaviour Difficulties

£10.00 • Paperback • 64 A4 pages • 1-84312-228-6 • July 2004

Supporting Children with Motor Co-ordination Difficulties

£10.00 • Paperback • 64 A4 pages • 1-84312-227-8 • July 2004

Supporting Children with Fragile X Syndrome

£10.00 • Paperback • 64 A4 pages • 1-84312-226-X • July 2004

Supporting Children with Speech and Language Difficulties

£10.00 • Paperback • 144 A4 pages • 1-84312-225-1 • July 2004

Supporting Children with Medical Conditions

£20.00 • Paperback • 144 A4 pages • 1-84312-224-3 • May 2004

Supporting Children with Epilepsy

£10.00 • Paperback • 64 A4 pages • 1-84312-223-5 • May 2004

Supporting Children with Dyslexia

£10.00 • Paperback • 48 A4 pages • 1-84312-222-7 • July 2004

Supporting Children with Down's Syndrome

£10.00 • Paperback • 48 A4 pages • 1-84312-221-9 • May 2004

Supporting Children with Cerebral Palsy

£10.00 • Paperback • 48 A4 pages • 1-84312-220-0 • May 2004

Supporting Children with Autistic Spectrum Disorder

£10.00 • Paperback • 64 A4 pages • 1-84312-219-7 • May 2004

Supporting Children with Asthma

£10.00 • Paperback • 48 A4 pages • 1-84312-218-9 • May 2004

ORDER FORM

Qty	ISBN	Title	Price	Subtotal
	1-84312-218-9	Supporting Children with Asthma	£10.00	
	1-84312-219-7	Supporting Children with ASD	£10.00	
	1-84312-228-6	Supporting Children with Behaviour Ds	£10.00	
	1-84312-220-0	Supporting Children with Cerebral Palsy	£10.00	
	1-84312-221-9	Supporting Children with Down's Syndrome	£10.00	
	1-84312-222-7	Supporting Children with Dyslexia	£10.00	
	1-84312-223-5	Supporting Children with Epilepsy	£10.00	
	1-84312-226-X	Supporting Children with Fragile X Syndrome	£10.00	
	1-84312-224-3	Supporting Children with Medical Conditions	£20.00	
	1-84312-227-8	Supporting Children with MCDs	£10.00	
	1-84312-225-1	Supporting Children with S&L Difficulties	£10.00	
	1-84312-204-9	David Fulton Catalogue	FREE	

Postage and Packing: FREE to schools, LEAs and other institutions.
£2.50 per order for private/personal orders.
Prices and publication dates are subject to change.

P&P	
TOTAL	

Please complete delivery details:

Name: ....

Organisation: ....

....

Address: ....

....

....

....

Postcode:..

Tel: ....

Email: ....

☐   Please add me to your email mailing list

Payment:

☐   Please invoice *(applicable to schools, LEAs and other institutions)*

☐   I enclose a cheque payable to David Fulton Publishers Ltd *(include postage and packing if applicable)*

☐   Please charge to my credit card *(Visa/Barclaycard, Access/Mastercard, American Express, Switch, Delta)*

card number ☐☐☐☐☐☐☐☐☐☐☐☐☐☐☐☐☐☐☐

expiry date ☐☐☐☐

(Switch customers only) valid from ☐☐☐☐   issue number ☐

Send your order to our distributors:

HarperCollins Publishers
Customer Service Centre
Westerhill Road • Bishopbriggs
Glasgow • G64 2QT

Tel. 0870 787 1721

Fax. 0870 787 1723

or order online at
www.fultonpublishers.co.uk